You Have the Power to: Rebuild Your Life, Relationships & Marriage

M. M. KIRSCHBAUM, RN-BC, CMSRN

You Have the Power to: Rebuild Your Life, Relationships & Marriage

DEDICATION

"I AM THAT I AM," that is His Name forever. There is none like Him. From everlasting to everlasting, He remains GOD! Father, take all the glory, honor, adoration, victory, my LORD, my KING, my Savior, my Love and my Redeemer!

CONTENTS

ACKNOWLEDGMENTS

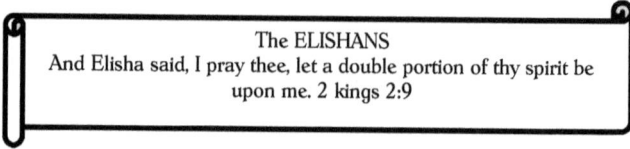

The ELISHANS
And Elisha said, I pray thee, let a double portion of thy spirit be upon me. 2 kings 2:9

www.Biblegateway.com - The Holy Bible, King James Version

http://www.doverpublications.com – Royal-Free images

www.purpleartstudios.com – Abraham

Names of families changed – thank you for sharing.

All Scripture quotations derived from: The Holy Bible, King James Version

Chapter One
SUDDENLY, THE PHONE RINGS

The phone-call came about 2 a.m. It was from Florence and she was crying. The issue concerned her husband, John. In the last three weeks ago, she lost her job and faced escalating family pressure. Special care was necessary for John who had daily dialysis sessions. This is a tedious system of removing impurities, wastes from the blood due to the inability of the kidneys to function properly. It was the only technique available to help remove toxins from his body. This is, a continuous and complicated procedure demanding constant monitoring and support. Florence requested prayers from the Elishans prayer group, believers of the double–portion anointing.

There was constant worry that, he could develop some infection, bleeding from the site of procedure-access or air embolism. For those familiar with this procedure, anticipatory instructions can be cumbersome and sensitive issues related to sexuality, can be a source of humiliation.

But, this phone-call from Florence had nothing to do with dialysis but plenty to do with emotional disappointment. She discovered that, John had rekindled his relationship with an old flame. She could not comprehend his actions with their present situation. There was no rhyme or quatrain. She asked him and he confessed! She could not imagine this extent of betrayal.

"How can the just live by faith? I cannot go on like this and how dare John cheat?" she demanded.

We prayed together on the phone. In challenging times, such as this one, we must continue to trust in the LORD of HOST. God does not lie. He is the same yesterday, today, and forever. He is omnipotent, omniscience, omnipresent, the great Shepherd. Even, as we prayed, we knew that, God will not fail. The means and how was not for us to determine. Skipping dinner, we prayed, seeking the face of God, our Maker.

Life is war and battles must be fought constantly. We cannot afford to lose so, we picked a weapon. The Spirit of the Lord led us to the book of prophet Isaiah Chapters 36 and 37. Understand this: God does not change. The Holy Bible is infallible, unerring, goofproof and teeming with guide lights

along the pathway of life. God's words will not fail.
One day, the kings, queens, celebrities, beauties, sex-
symbols, trillion-millionaires making waves will pass
away. They will become history and all they own will
be taken over by others but the word of God will
remain true from everlasting to everlasting! All the
arrogance of heart will be humbled and their deeds
will be wind and confusion but God will remain true
to those who place their trust in Him.

"Now it came to pass in the fourteenth year
of King Hezekiah, that Sennacherib king of Assyria
came up against all the defensed cities of Judah, and
took them. And the king of Assyria sent Rabshakeh
from Lachish to Jerusalem unto King Hezekiah with
a great army. And he stood by the conduit of the
upper pool in the highway of the fuller's field which
was over the house, and Shebna the scribe, and Joah,
Asaph's son, the recorder.

And Rabshakeh said unto them, Say ye now
to Hezekiah, Thus saith the great king, the king of
Assyria, What confidence is this wherein thou
trustest? I have counsel and strength for war: now
on whom dost thou trust, that thou rebel against
me? Lo, thou trustest in the staff of this broken reed,
on Egypt; whereon if a man leans, it will go into his
hand, and pierce it: so is Pharaoh king of Egypt to all
that trust in him. But if thou say to me, we trust in

the LORD our God: is it not he, whose high places and whose altars Hezekiah hath taken away, and said to Judah and to Jerusalem, Ye shall worship before this altar? master the king of Assyria, and I will give thee two thousand horses, if thou be able on thy part to set riders upon them. How then wilt thou turn away the face of one captain of the least of my master's servants, and put thy trust on Egypt for chariots and for horsemen? And am I now come up without the LORD against this land to destroy it? the LORD said unto me, Go up against this land, and destroy it. Then said Eliakim and Shebna and Joah unto Rabshakeh, Speak, I pray thee, unto thy servants in the Syrian language; for we understand it: and speak not to us in the Jews' language, in the ears of the people that are on the wall. But Rabshakeh said, Hath my master sent me to thy master and to thee to speak these words? hath he not sent me to the men that sit upon the wall, that they may eat their own dung, and drink their own piss with you?

Then Rabshakeh stood, and cried with a loud voice in the Jews' language, and said, Hear ye the words of the great king, the king of Assyria. Thus saith the king, Let not Hezekiah deceives you: for he shall not be able to deliver you. Neither let Hezekiah make you trust in the LORD, saying, The LORD will surely deliver us: this city shall not be

delivered into the hand of the king of Assyria.
Hearken not to Hezekiah: for thus saith the
king of Assyria, Make an agreement with me by a
present, and come out to me: and eat ye every one of
his vine, and every one of his fig tree, and drink ye
every one the waters of his own cistern; Until I come
and take you away to a land like your own land, a
land of corn and wine, a land of bread and vineyards.
Beware lest Hezekiah persuade you, saying, the
LORD will deliver us. Hath any of the gods of the
nations delivered his land out of the hand of the
king of Assyria? Where are the gods of Hamath and
Arphad? are the gods of Sepharvaim? and have they
delivered Samaria out of my hand? Who are they
among all the gods of these lands that have
delivered their land out of my hand, that the LORD
should deliver Jerusalem out of my hand? But they
held their peace, and answered him not a word: for
the king's commandment was, saying, Answer him
not.

Then came Eliakim, the son of Hilkiah, that was
over the household, and Shebna the scribe, and Joah,
the son of Asaph, the recorder, to Hezekiah with
their clothes rent, and told him the words of
Rabshakeh And it came to pass, when king Hezekiah
heard it, that he rent his clothes, and covered himself
with sackcloth, and went into the house of the
LORD. And he sent Eliakim, who was over the

household, and Shebna the scribe, and the elders of the priests covered with sackcloth, unto Isaiah the prophet the son of Amoz. And they said unto him, Thus saith Hezekiah, This day is a day of trouble, and of rebuke, and of blasphemy: for the children are come to the birth, and there is not strength to bring forth. It may be the LORD thy God will hear the words of Rabshakeh, whom the king of Assyria his master hath sent to reproach the living God, and will reprove the words which the LORD thy God hath heard: wherefore lift up thy prayer for the remnant that is left.

So the servants of king Hezekiah came to Isaiah. And Isaiah said unto them, Thus shall ye say unto your master, Thus saith the LORD, Be not afraid of the words that thou hast heard, wherewith the servants of the king of Assyria have blasphemed me. Behold, I will send a blast upon him, and he shall hear a rumor, and return to his own land; and I will cause him to fall by the sword in his own land. So Rabshakeh returned, and found the king of Assyria warring against Libnah: for he had heard that he was departed from Lachish. And he heard say concerning Tirhakah king of Ethiopia, He is come forth to make war with thee."

In Jesus name, they that war against you shall hear rumors and turn from you – amen!

Chapter TWO
ABILITY TO COMPREHEND

The power of God is your protection and His knowledge is too wonderful for us to comprehend. We cannot grasp it. Our mind has no track or profile to measure it.

According to, Psalm 139 from verses 9 to10, the psalmist attempt to metaphorical explains the concept.

"If I take the wings of the morning, and dwell in the uttermost parts of the sea, even there Your hand shall lead me, and Your right hand shall hold me" God is everywhere and will establish and accomplish His purposes through mankind.

God will have mercy on you and give you rest from your anxiety in the name of Jesus, amen.

And Hezekiah received the letter from the hand messengers, and read it: and Hezekiah went up unto the house of the LORD, and spread it before the LORD.

And Hezekiah prayed unto the LORD, saying,

"O LORD of hosts, God of Israel, that dwellest between the cherubims, thou art the God, even thou alone, of all the kingdoms of the earth: thou hast made heaven and earth. Incline thine ear, O LORD, and hear; open thine eyes, O LORD, and see: and see: and hear all the words of Sennacherib, which hath sent to reproach the living God. Of a truth, LORD, the kings of Assyria have laid waste all the nations, and their countries, And have cast their gods into the fire: for they were no gods, but the work of men's hands, wood and stone: therefore they have destroyed them. Now therefore, O LORD our God, save us from his hand, that all the kingdoms of the earth may know that thou art the LORD, even thou only."

This prayer is as true then and remains true today. Many of us have a, "Sennacherib king of Assyria," in their life. The person that, despises you and laugh you to scorn. You cannot fight them alone nor can you fight what you do not comprehend. If you place the issue before the Lord, then God will strike back on your behalf.

Observe God's reply to king Hezekiah:

"Whom hast thou reproached and blasphemed? and

against whom hast thou exalted thy voice, and lifted up thine eyes on high? even against the Holy One of Israel. By thy servants hast thou reproached the Lord, and hast said, By the multitude of my chariots am I come up to the height of the mountains, to the sides of Lebanon; and I will cut down the tall cedars thereof, and the choice fir trees thereof: and I will enter into the height of his border, and the forest of his Carmel. I have digged, and drunk water; and with the sole of my feet have I dried up all the rivers of the besieged places. Hast thou not heard long ago, how I have done it; and of ancient times, that I have formed it? now have I brought it to pass, that thou shouldest be to lay waste defenced cities into ruinous heaps. Therefore their inhabitants were of small power, they were dismayed and confounded: they were as the grass of the field, and as the green herb, as the grass on the housetops, and as corn blasted before it be grown up. But I know thy abode, and thy going out, and thy coming in, and thy rage against me. Because thy rage against me, and thy tumult, is come up into mine ears, therefore will I put my hook in thy nose, and my bridle in thy lips, and I will turn thee back by the way by which thou camest. The zeal of the LORD of hosts shall do this."

In the mighty name of Jesus, God shall put a hook unto those that contend with you, amen.

This is an unending prohercy, "Therefore thus saith the LORD concerning the king of Assyria, He shall not come into this city, nor shoot an arrow there, nor come before it with shields, nor cast a bank against it. By the way that he came, by the same shall he return, and shall not come into this city, saith the LORD. For I will defend this city to save it for mine own sake, and for my servant David's sake."

Then the angel of the LORD went forth, and smote in the camp of the Assyrians a hundred and fourscore and five thousand: and when they arose early in the morning, behold, they were all dead corpses. So Sennacherib king of Assyria departed, and went and returned, and dwelt at Nineveh.

And it came to pass, as he was worshipping in the house of Nisroch his god, that Adrammelech and Sharezer his sons smote him with the sword; and they escaped into the land of Armenia: and Esarhaddon his son reigned in his stead.
God is a great God to serve!

Back to the case of Florence. By the dawn of the fourth day of prayer, she was surprised to see her father-in-law. He was at their door-step and this was the first time. He lived as a recluse and would not even visit any family or show interest in his grandchildren. Pleasantly surprised, Florence continue to thank God. He promised to support them and ease the task of taking John for dialysis, twice a week. We give God all the glory because God is merciful, His way is far from our ways.

Thus, I pray with you that, in Jesus name, the Sennacheribs and the king of Assyria in your life, marriage or relationship will depart. They shall return back to the same way they came. When, they go back to worship their gods, their evil shall smote them in the name of Jesus amen. Take this prayer intentions wholeheartedly and believe.

The Lord will visit you in challenging times and he will not let you be disgraced, amen.

1. My God, the Creator of all things visible and invisible, I beg for forgiveness related to ......(Mention) in the name of Jesus.
2. God of my salvation, hide me under your wings for you are the Lord of my life. I will exalt you above all things for you are my EL SHADDAI, the GREAT PROVIDER.
3. You are my light and my Savior; whom shall I fear? You are the defender of my life; of whom shall I be afraid? Have pity on me, and hearken to my request regarding ......in the name of Jesus.

CHAPTER THREE
DEALING WITH THE SEASON OF DOUBT

There is a season of doubt. God is all-powerful because He can exalt and He cast down. He manifest His love by sending His only-begotten Son that if may believe. In the book of Isaiah Chapter 55, He assures us:

"As the rain cometh down, and the snow from heaven, and returneth not thither, but watereth the earth and maketh it bring forth and bud that it may give seed to the sower and bread to the eater, so Shalt My Word be that goeth forth out of My mouth: it shall not return unto Me void, but it shall accomplish that which I please and it shall prosper in the thing whereto I sent it." the significance of this is to reveal God's righteousness, for our faith is based on this power.

So, seeking first the kingdom of God and His righteousness is really placing one in the hands of mercy and asking for help. God is merciful, far beyond our comprehension. Let us examine the story of King Asa in the second book of Chronicles chapter 14.

"So Abijah slept with his fathers, and they buried him in the city of David: and Asa his son reigned in his stead. In his days the land was quiet ten years. And Asa did that which was good and right in the eyes of the LORD his God: For he took away the altars of the strange gods, and the high places, and brake down the images, and cut down the groves:

And commanded Judah to seek the LORD God of their fathers, and to do the law and the commandment. Also he took away out of all the cities of Judah the high places and the images: and the kingdom was quiet before him. And he built fenced cities in Judah: for the land had rest and he had no war in those years; because the LORD had given him rest. Therefore he said unto Judah, Let us build these cities, and make about them walls, and towers, gates, and bars, while the land is yet before us; because we have sought the LORD our God, we have sought him, and he hath given us rest on every side. So they built and prospered. And Asa had an army of men that bare targets and spears, out of Judah three hundred thousand; and out of Benjamin, that bare shields and drew bows, two hundred and fourscore thousand: all these were mighty men of valour.

And there came out against them Zerah the Ethiopian with an host of a thousand, and three hundred chariots; and came unto Mareshah. Then Asa went out against him, and they set the battle in array in the valley of Zephathah at Mareshah. And Asa cried unto the LORD his God, and said, LORD, it is nothing with thee to help, whether with many, or with them that have no power: help us, O LORD our God; for we rest on thee, and in thy name we go against this multitude. O LORD, thou art our God; let not man prevail against thee. So the LORD smote the Ethiopians before Asa, and before Judah; and the Ethiopians fled. And Asa and the people that were with him pursued them unto Gerar: and the Ethiopians were overthrown, that they could not recover themselves; for they were destroyed before the LORD, and before his host; and they carried away very much spoil. And they smote all the cities round about Gerar; for the fear of the LORD came upon them: and they spoiled all the cities; for there was exceeding much spoil in them. They smote also the tents of cattle, and carried away sheep and camels in abundance, and returned to Jerusalem."

God will strike fear in your enemies, in Jesus name, amen. King Asa trusted God when enemies overwhelmed him. At one time or another we were out-numbered by issues. Faithfulness to God brings reward. Stand your ground when trouble attempts to overtake your relationship or your marriage. When situations arise that tempt our will, seek the Lord's face. Where is that person who will say: "O LORD, thou art my God; I will exalt thee, I will praise thy name; for thou hast done wonderful things; thy counsels of old are faithfulness and truth. For thou hast made of a city a heap; of a defensed city a ruin: a palace of strangers to be no city; it shall never be built. Therefore shall the strong people glorify thee, the city of the terrible nations shall fear thee."

No, it is not Disney world, it is real. Remain standing, remain strong, and believe! God will strengthen you. He will be a refuge to you from the storm, a shadow from the heat in the name of Jesus, amen. God will blast those who terrify you as a storm against the wall and bring down the noise of strangers, as the heat in a dry place in the name of Jesus. Indeed, the branch of the terrible ones shall be brought low.

If your case is similar, take note that, you will never be ashamed. If, "the Lord GOD will help me; who is he that shall condemn you? Lo, they all shall wax old as a garment; the moth shall eat them up," in Jesus name, amen. King Asa was faced with annihilation, he said. "LORD, it is nothing for You to help, whether with many or with those who have no power; help us, O LORD our God, for we rest on You, and in Your name we go against this multitude. O LORD, You are our God; do not let man prevail against You!"

CHAPTER FOUR
LET US REASON TOGETHER

Johnson sat by the bedside, praying and pleading to God. His one request was in front of him. His only son James was in the Emergency Room/Intensive Care Unit of a hospital. He was being monitored for unstable life-threatening injury sustained in school. The primary survey of airway, breathing, circulation initiated simultaneous cervical spine stabilization. His father wished to be present and actively participate in the care process.

At this moment, Johnson remained shocked, in disbelief and denial with very frightening questioning. The inability to think and process his emotional response is another source of panic escalating the feeling of disintegration.

Looking at his 10 year old son, who would believe that, four hours ago he was having a bowl of cereal and preparing for school? It was an accident on the play field, unexpected, sudden but casting a dark cloud. If only, Joyce was picking-up her cell phone. Their recent, frequent arguments leaped to flinching pitch as they looked at each other with flaming hatred. With nostalgia, Johnson can pin the time when their relationship manifested downhearted low. Since the promotion at work, her priority changed to opposite direction. It was no longer family but her well-toned, divorced supervisor. Life, as he suddenly swapped positions. Joyce would dress and fix her hair as, "the supervisor likes it." The variation in the economy did not alleviate the situation at home. They have become strangers to each other.

Inconceivable and implausible to their in-laws, they live in the same house, have two great children, use the same kitchen, bathroom and sleep on the same bed.

Just then, the medical team walked into the room. They whispered between themselves and asked if he was the father. As they stepped out, he knew it! Soon, extended family members would begin to trickle into the hospital room. There is little space and no answers. He could hear the humming of low-tone of the complex, life-saving machines.

Reluctantly, Johnson surveyed the connecting tubes and his heart pounded harder. "Where is Joyce?" She should be on the other side of the bed, holding their son's other hand. At this moment, he was ready to do anything for a hug, a whisper from his wife, friend and love.

Johnson was suffering from, "Hidden Burden syndrome." You will not find it in a dictionary but it exists. This is, when an issue is difficult to integrate or explain. The effectiveness of coping strategies cannot be readily identified. The person affected cannot share their issues with a care provider even as the degree of anxiety escalates.

Only the presence of a trusted person can alleviate the attack based on communicating deepest feelings. Nobody can understand the burden as the spirit cries out for help.

In the book of Isaiah chapter 1: verses 18 to 20.

"Come now, and let us reason together, saith the LORD: though your sins be as scarlet, they shall be as white as snow; though they be red like crimson, they shall be as wool. If ye be willing and obedient, ye shall eat the good of the land:
But if ye refuse and rebel, ye shall be devoured with the sword: for the mouth of the LORD hath spoken it."
Our heavenly Father understands our needs. His name is, Jehovah-Jireh because He is the Provider.

Isaac said to Abraham in the book of Genesis, "Behold the fire and the wood, but where is the lamb for a burnt offering?" God will provide and will not fail in that season of need.

Johnson decided that it was time to accept the Lord Jesus whose precious blood was shed on the cross. the plan of salvation is light upon the throne of the Most High. Jesus gave himself willingly. He carried the load of sin on His shoulders by eclipsing the fall of the first Adam.

Oh, how wonderful for God is perfect. The word of the LORD is tried, sure and certain. In the book of Psalms Chapter 7 from verses 1:

"O Lord my God, in thee do I put my trust: save me from all them that persecute me, and deliver me."

I pray that, in the mighty name of Jesus you will say boldly according to the psalmist:

"In the LORD put I my trust: How say ye to my soul, Flee as a bird to your mountain? Preserve me, O God: for in thee do I put my trust. The LORD is my rock, and my fortress, and my deliverer; my God, my strength, in whom I will trust; my buckler, and the horn of my salvation, and my high tower. Some trust in chariots, and some in horses: but we will remember the name of the LORD our God."

How excellent is God's loving-kindness, let us place our trust under the shadow of His wings.

In the book of Ezekiel, chapter 13: in brief, "And say, Thus faith the Lord GOD; Woe to the women that sew pillows to all armholes, and make kerchiefs upon the head of every stature to hunt souls! Will ye hunt the souls of my people, and will ye save the souls alive that come unto you? 19And will ye pollute me among my people for handfuls of barley and for pieces of bread, to slay the souls that should not die, and to save the souls alive that should not live, by your lying to my people that hear your lies? 20Wherefore thus faith the Lord GOD; Behold, I am against your pillows, wherewith ye there hunt the souls to make them fly, and I will tear them from your arms, and will let the souls go, even the souls that ye hunt to make them fly."

Let us re-examine, the invasion of Sennacherib in 2 Kings chapters 18 and 19. Sennacherib king of Assyria came up against all the defensed cities of Judah, and took them. He already 'took' the defense cities. Subsequently, the king of Assyria sent a message to king Hezekiah. Well, the messenger came with a large army and decided to deliver it via the most public/open. The message was an arrogant taunt and ridicule. It was an affront of, 'on what or who do you place your trust?'

From verses 5 to 20: "Do you think that mere words are strategy and power for war? In whom do you now trust that you have rebelled against me? - Behold, you are trusting in Egypt, that broken reed of a staff, which will pierce the hand of any man who leans on it. ... Come now, make a wager with my master the king of Assyria: I will give you two thousand horses, if you are able on your part to set riders on them. How then can you repulse a single captain among the least of my master's servants,

when you trust in Egypt for chariots and for horsemen? Moreover, is it without the LORD that I have come up against this land to destroy it? The LORD said to me, Go up against this land and destroy it….Do not let Hezekiah deceive you, for he will not be able to deliver you. Do not let Hezekiah make you trust in the LORD by saying, "The LORD will surely deliver us. This city will not be given into the hand of the king of Assyria."
Simple translation: "Compromise or die."
Can you imagine this condition? To be told, "Who are they among all the gods of these lands that have delivered their land out of my hand, that the LORD should deliver Jerusalem out of my hand?"

We are told that, "they held their peace, and answered him not a word: for the king's commandment was, Answer him not". In the next chapter, the story unfolds to the next step. "King Hezekiah heard it, and he tore his clothes and covered himself with sackcloth and went into the house of the LORD."

This must have being an ominous and frightful period. The king made a decision. He turned to the Lord. He humbled himself and all his officials, their households, senior priests and the Prophet Isaiah. In verses 3 to 4, "They said to him, "Thus says Hezekiah, 'This day is a day of distress, of rebuke, and of disgrace; children have come to the point of birth, and there is no strength to bring them forth."

Be Encouraged...I pray that it shall be well with you, there is hope. God will wipe your tears; do not be frightened, you will succeed in the mighty name of Jesus. Be encouraged. decide to fast from a meal each day.

CHAPTER FIVE
A TIME TO PRAY

It is time to pray.

God says:

"Fear thou not; for I am with thee: be not dismayed; for I am thy God: I will strengthen thee; yea, I will help thee; yea, I will uphold thee with the right hand of my righteousness. Behold, all they that were incensed against thee shall be ashamed and confounded: they shall be as nothing; and they that strive with thee shall perish. Thou shalt seek them, and shalt not find them, even them that contended with thee: they that war against thee shall be as nothing, and as a thing of nought. For I the LORD thy God will hold thy right hand, saying unto thee, Fear not; I will help thee. For I beheld, and there was no man; even among them, and there was no counsellor, that, when I asked of them, could answer a word. Behold, they are all vanity; their works are nothing: their molten images are wind and confusion." Isaiah Chapter 41.

Plan according to what works for you, consider your circumstances. My friend, Susan decided to consume fruits for lunch and dinner. At the end of the session, she lost few pounds and the husband was even the first to compliment her. Plan, organize yourself and consider any of your prescribed medications. A friend decided to pre-make the family dinner, label them and have them frozen neatly. She returned from work 30 minutes early in order to, have the opportunity of privacy.

God is not hidden and He remains the Almighty, the all-knowing, the beginning and the end. He shall hear your prayer and grant your heart's petition by the name of Jesus, amen.

Let us give thanks to God. Pray and you will see supernatural power in action. Do not be afraid, stand still and see the goodness of the Lord. The LORD will fight for you because all things are possible to Him. He will lift you up above the circumstance. God is still in the business of deliverance. He is a Father, who wishes His children well.

Let us give Him glory and He is still the great provider. I pray this day that God will open your eyes and understanding in your endeavors in the name of Jesus, Amen.

Hezekiah's Prayer for Deliverance

"O LORD of hosts, God of Israel, enthroned above the cherubim, you are the God, you alone, of all the kingdoms of the earth; you have made heaven and earth. Incline your ear, O LORD, and hear; open your eyes, O LORD, and see; and hear all the words of Sennacherib, which he has sent to mock the living God. Truly, O LORD, the kings of Assyria have laid waste all the nations and their lands, and have cast their gods into the fire. For they were no gods, but the work of men's hands, wood and stone. Therefore they were destroyed. So now, O LORD our God, save us from his hand, that all the kingdoms of the earth may know that you alone are the LORD."

Did you catch this part of the prayer: "Truly, O LORD, the kings of Assyria have laid waste all the nations and their lands, and have cast their gods into the fire."

When a friend, Elian took a look at the picture of the husband's girlfriend, she crumbled to the floor. This lady was opposite of Elian. She was slim-looking, well-toned, tall and really, really full-head of hair. Yes, truly she look beautiful, younger and desirable. But, Elian had to change her prayer objectives and used this prayer objective to fight the battle.

King Hezekiah said, "For they were no gods, but the work of men's hands, wood and stone. Therefore they were destroyed. So now, O LORD our God, save us from his hand, that all the kingdoms of the earth may know that you alone are the LORD."

Just as suddenly as she came into their lives so did she abandon Elian's husband for a richer, younger guy. The husband lost face because the guy turned out to be his chairman's son. Humbled and afraid of losing his job, he confessed to Elian and promised to make his family a priority.

The zeal of the LORD of hosts will be with you in the name of Jesus, amen. Let us read God's reply again. What a sweet God to serve! "Therefore thus says the LORD concerning the king of Assyria: He shall not come into this city or shoot an arrow there or come before it with a shield or cast up a siege mound against it. By the way that he came, by the same he shall return, and he shall not come into this city, declares the LORD."

It is a challenge to resist the temptation of this world ensnared with distress and hazards. As a result, the psalmist cried to, the Lord for pity because beside him, there was no help. God is moved with compassion, he is faithful and keeps his covenant of love to a thousand generations of those who love him and keep his commands. There is no God like him in heaven or on earth. His love endures forever.

The LORD is slow to anger, abounding in love and forgiving sins. In Psalm 33, the eyes of the LORD are on those who fear him, on those whose hope is in his unfailing love.

In times of spiritual darkness encourage yourself in your Maker. Do not look to the left or right, because when we call, God hears! A sea of alcohol cannot dull the pain nor can time wipe out the pain we feel. Every season, time of year, period, incident reminds us that, we are human. We are dust and to dust we shall return. Therefore, I pray that you are strengthened in the Lord and the power of the Holy Spirit will make: "All things work together for the good." And you will be able to utter the words of Joseph. His brothers did evil by selling him as a slave but God meant it for good. Be hopeful - You are not alone, do not be despondent.

Let us talk about Jesus. He knew pain, he knew sorrow, he knew depression, he was betrayed, he was mocked, and he was pounded with trapping-questions all day. When he healed the sick, he was criticized, when he lifted the oppressed, he was condemned. When an exception displays gratitude, he was censored and suppressed. Even, some of His family members belittled him. He was sneered, scoffed and jeered in is environment. Yet, Jesus continued to heal the sick, raise the dead, forgive sins, feed the poor and accepted all who came to him. He suffered, died, rose and continues to manifest that same love to this day. He has not changed and he is faithful. He remains the Savior, Redeemer, Merciful Lord of Lords and King of Kings.

Jesus experienced loneliness, refutation, repudiation, denunciation in just three years of earthly ministry! So, what are you going through that, he does not understand? Do not look to others and seek manifestation of Jesus. No – do not lose hope. Just sit, stand, kneel or whatever and ask Jesus to help you. You may be reading this publication in a bathroom, car, dinning-place or bar – it does not matter.

Isa. 43:19: "Behold, I will do a new thing; now it shall spring forth; shall ye not know it? I will even make a way in the wilderness, and rivers in the desert."

As a society in a hurry, remaining still is a challenge. Temptations will surface which may come as anger, quarrel, fear, guilt etc. Pray anytime, anywhere, in the bathroom, in your car, walking, anywhere. God is everywhere and He will hear you in the name of Jesus. There is POWER in, the Blood of Jesus!

Let God be God! Call his name: Jesus! The name above all names. He will open your spirit and you will know that, "Jesus is the author and finisher of our faith, the Alpha and Omega." It cannot get simpler than this, it is free and you will not be condemned or judged.

PRAY

1. Lord, open my eyes that I may see in spirit and open my mind that I may understand my situation, in Jesus' name.

2. My God, You do not desire sacrifice but a broken spirit hear me now, by the name of Jesus.

3. My God, do not despise me; lift my burden off me for I am broken. I need you to .... (Mention your desire) in the name of Jesus.

CHAPTER SIX
YOU HAVE THE POWER

Session One

It is necessary to give thanks to God for everything. Now, ask for forgiveness from God (For example, my God, my Father I have done..........I know this is displeasing to you. Forgive me for the sake of your son, Jesus Christ. If you judge me or your children, who shall stand before your holy throne? Forgive me and my family in Jesus' name. You are the beginning and the end, the alpha and Omega. Be glorified; hear me, as I begin this prayer session in Jesus Name.) Psalm 51

Session 2

1. Have mercy upon me, O God, According to Your loving-kindness; According to the multitude of your tender mercies by the name of Jesus.

2.   Blot out my transgressions, wash me thoroughly from my iniquity; cleanse me from my sin by the name of Jesus.

3.   For I acknowledge my transgressions, my sins are always before me. Against You, You only, have I sinned, forgive me by the name of Jesus.

Session 3

1.   I was brought forth in iniquity, and in sin my mother conceived me therefore, purge me of hidden sins and I shall be clean by the name of Jesus.

2.   Wash me, and I shall be whiter than snow, hide your face from my sins and blot out all my iniquities by the name of Jesus.

Session 4

Repeat this forgiveness prayer if you feel burdened, Plead the blood of Jesus over yourself, family, body, soul and spirit. Continue to plead the blood, plead the blood of Jesus and say, "LET THE BLOOD OF JESUS CLEAN ME, REFRESH ME...............

Session 5

1.   Create in me a clean heart, let me hear joy and gladness in my home, by the name of Jesus.

3. Renew a steadfast spirit within me and do not cast me away from your presence, by the name of Jesus.

5. Do not take Your Holy Spirit from me and restore to me the joy of your salvation, in by the name of Jesus.

Session 6

1. Deliver me from the guilt of bloodshed, uphold me by your generous Spirit in by the name of Jesus.by the name of Jesus.

2. O God, You are the God of my salvation, deliver me completely by the name of Jesus.

3. Let my tongue sing aloud of your righteousness by the name of Jesus.

In Isaiah chapter 40, Every valley shall be exalted, and every mountain and hill shall be made low: and the crooked shall be made straight, and the rough places plain: And the glory of the LORD shall be revealed, and all flesh shall see it together: for the mouth of the LORD hath spoken it.

We have to let God be God. When we limit His power, we deprive ourselves of the goodness of God as a father. Place your trust in Him. In some instances, things may not turn-out as we envisage it but He will never fail.

Isaiah 31 from verses 1 to 6: "Woe to them that go down to Egypt for help; and stay on horses, and trust in chariots, because they are many; and in horsemen, because they are very strong; but they look not unto the Holy One of Israel, neither seek the LORD! Yet he also is wise, and will bring evil, and will not call back his words: but will arise against the house of the evildoers, and against the help of them that work iniquity. Now the Egyptians are men, and not God; and their horses flesh, and not spirit. When the LORD shall stretch out his hand, both he that helped shall fall, and he that is helped shall fall down, and they all shall fail together."

CHAPTER SEVEN
HAVE FAITH

Have faith, be confident, and believe. God has not given us spirit of fear but of power, of sound mind and of love. God will empower you and you will be victorious, in Jesus' name. God will manifest His power in your case, even if you do not believe or understand. For every day, it is critical to thank God for His goodness. Remember that, there are many things happening that we know nothing about. How about what we do not see?

Today, you are alive and there is hope. To God be the glory for, He will give you victory and turn your tears to laughter in Jesus name, amen. Do not lose faith, understandably, these are challenging times but God is in control. Pains of the past will hurt but you must now learn to examine and re-examine the incredible blessings as well. According to, Proverbs chapter 3, verse 5, "Trust in the Lord with all your heart, and lean not on your own understanding; in all your ways acknowledge Him, and He shall direct your paths."

In Isaiah, there is a promise that of perfect peace. Blessed is the person who trusts in the Lord, and whose hope is the Lord. You will overcome anxiousness, apprehension or agitation. In Jesus name, God will direct your paths and you will prosper. Remain steadfast in the Lord as you go through this 3-day prayer session.

Do not lose hope. God is omnipotent, omnipresent and you will be successful in Jesus name, amen. Be not afraid. The possibilities of God are beyond our comprehension.

Be confident because God has not given us spirit of fear but of power, of sound mind and of love. God will empower you and you will be victorious, in Jesus' name. He will manifest His power in your case, there are many things happening that we know nothing about. We only complain of what we see.

Today, God will give you victory and turn your tears to laughter. During this period, be patient. You have the power to supernaturally make it happen. God will not abandon you nor forsake you.

Session One
Y   Begin by pleading the blood of Jesus over you, body, soul and spirit. Plead, plead the blood

of Jesus. Be bold because Jesus did not shed His
blood in vain.

Y   Ask God to forgive you for whatever
burdens you – in the name of Jesus. Ask God to
open up your understanding to secret things
related to your relationship/marriage.

Y   Ask God to reveal any secret behind the
failing marriage and let the Holy Spirit expose the
truth in any form. This could be through dreams,
an individual, letter, intuition or a connection to
something or someone.

Session Two

Y   Ask for divine wisdom to handle the
truth and to make the right decision.

Y   Pray that, every cloud preventing you
from seeing or understanding the situation to be
cleared. You want to know, you need spiritual
vision and understanding the power in the blood
of Jesus.

Session 3

Y   Pray for supernatural and extraordinary
divine intervention, in the name of Jesus.

Y   Pray that, the fire of God should melt
and confuse any limitation and every root of
failure, despair in the name of Jesus.

Y   Pray that, God should arise and guide you into the mysteries of life that will help you in re-constructing your relationship/marriage.

Session 4

Y   Pray: call every imagination, external interferences, and any extra-marital connection/affairs in any form bluff, in Jesus name.

Y   Pray that, every unhappiness, external stress disturbing you be dissolve by the blood of Jesus.

The word of God concerning your life, marriage, and career is settled in heaven and no one or thing has power or authority over your happiness in Jesus name.

Every thought of hopelessness, helplessness and frustration will be cancelled in the name of Jesus.

Do not limit God. You have the power. Be hopeful. Is there anything too difficult for God to do? It will be well with you because you are a child of the Most High God! Continue to pray without ceasing any place, anytime. For our Father is accessible to as our breath.

"Behold, the Lord GOD will come with strong hand, and his arm shall rule for him:

behold, his reward is with him, and his work
before him. He shall feed his flock like a
shepherd: he shall gather the lambs with his arm,
and carry them in his bosom, and shall gently
lead those that are with young. Who hath
measured the waters in the hollow of his hand,
and meted out heaven with the span, and
comprehended the dust of the earth in a measure,
and weighed the mountains in scales, and the
hills in a balance?

Who hath directed the Spirit of the LORD, or
being his counsellor hath taught him? With
whom took he counsel, and who instructed him,
and taught him in the path of judgment, and
taught him knowledge, and shewed to him the
way of understanding? Behold, the nations are as
a drop of a bucket, and are counted as the small
dust of the balance: behold, he taketh up the isles
as a very little thing. And Lebanon is not
sufficient to burn, nor the beasts thereof
sufficient for a burnt offering.

All nations before him are as nothing; and they
are counted to him less than nothing, and vanity.
To whom then will ye liken God? or what
likeness will ye compare unto him? The
workman melteth a graven image, and the
goldsmith spreadeth it over with gold, and
casteth silver chains. He that is so impoverished

that he hath no oblation chooseth a tree that will not rot; he seeketh unto him a cunning workman to prepare a graven image, that shall not be moved."

I pray that the Holy Spirit will strengthen you, in the name of Jesus. God will send His angels to lift you up, in the name of Jesus. Surely, goodness and mercy shall follow you all the rest of your life in name of Jesus.

Believe, have faith and it shall be well with you, in Jesus name – amen. It is not an accident that you are reading this – it shall be well with you, in the name of Jesus. I believe you will manifest your power - in Jesus name. Do not cry or feel defeated. May God hear your prayers and enrich your utterances and knowledge in Jesus' name. Is there anything too difficult for God to do?

"The word is near you; it is in your mouth and in your heart," with the mouth confession is made unto salvation. Have faith; there is great power in the spoken word of faith! Continue to fire rounds of prayer bombs on the issue and let it explode on whatever evil agent/agents interfering with your life.

Because you have made the LORD, who is my (your) refuge, Even the Most High, your dwelling place. No evil shall befall you, nor shall

any plague come near your dwelling; For He shall
give His angels charge over you, to keep you in
all your ways (Psalm 127, KJV)

CHAPTER EIGHTH
IT IS SETTLED

My dear reader, It shall be well with you in Jesus name, be not afraid!

Let God be exalted. This publication is dedicated to:

"I AM THAT I AM," that is His Name forever. There is none like Him. From everlasting to everlasting, He remains GOD! Father, take all the glory, honor, adoration, and victory, my LORD, my KING, my Savior, my Love and my Redeemer!

You are blessed because in Psalm 119,

"Blessed are the undefiled in the way, who walk in the law of the LORD. Blessed are they that keep his testimonies, and that seek him with the whole heart. They also do no iniquity: they walk in his ways."

The LORD will not count your iniquities against you in Jesus name. Accept Jesus into your life. Then you can say, "With my whole heart have I sought thee: O let me not wander from thy commandments. Thy word have I hid in mine heart, that I might not sin against thee. Blessed art thou, O LORD: teach me thy statutes. With my lips have I declared all the judgments of thy mouth. I have rejoiced in the way of thy testimonies, as much as in all riches. I will meditate in thy precepts, and have respect unto thy ways. I will delight myself in thy statutes: I will not forget thy word. Deal bountifully with thy servant, that I may live, and keep thy word. Open thou mine eyes, that I may behold wondrous things out of thy law. I am a stranger in the earth: hide not thy commandments from me."

In Isaiah 45, God said:

"I will go before thee, and make the crooked places straight: I will break in pieces the gates of brass, and cut in sunder the bars of iron: And I will give thee the treasures of darkness, and hidden riches of secret places, that thou mayest know that I, the LORD, which call thee by thy name, am the God of Israel."

"I am the LORD, and there is none else, there is no God beside me: I girded thee, though thou hast not known me: That they may know from the rising of the sun, and from the west, that there is none beside me. I am the LORD, and there is none else. I form the light, and create darkness: I make peace, and create evil: I the LORD do all these things. Drop down, ye heavens, from above, and let the skies pour down righteousness: let the earth open, and let them bring forth salvation, and let righteousness spring up together; I the LORD have created it."

"Look unto me, and be ye saved, all the ends of the earth: for I am God, and there is none else. I have sworn by myself, the word is gone out of my mouth in righteousness, and shall not return, That unto me every knee shall bow, every tongue shall swear."

In 2 Kings Chapter 3: "So the king of Israel went, and the king of Judah, and the king of Edom: and they fetched a compass of seven days' journey: and there was no water for the host, and for the cattle that followed them. And the king of Israel said, Alas! That the LORD hath called these three kings together, to deliver them into the hand of Moab! But Jehoshaphat said, Is there not here a prophet of the LORD, that we may enquire of the LORD by him? And one of the kings of Israel's servants answered and said, here is Elisha the son of Shaphat, which poured water on the hands of Elijah. And Jehoshaphat said, the word of the LORD is with him. So the king of Israel and Jehoshaphat and the king of Edom went down to him. And Elisha said unto the king of Israel, What have I to do with thee? Get thee to the prophets of thy father, and to the prophets of thy mother. And the king of Israel said unto

him, nay: for the LORD hath called these three
kings together, to deliver them into the hand of
Moab. And Elisha said, as the LORD of hosts
liveth, before whom I stand, surely, were it not
that I regard the presence of Jehoshaphat the
king of Judah, I would not look toward thee, nor
see thee. But now bring me a minstrel. And it
came to pass, when the minstrel played, that the
hand of the LORD came upon him. And he said,
Thus saith the LORD, Make this valley full of
ditches. For thus saith the LORD, Ye shall not
see wind, neither shall ye see rain; yet that valley
shall be filled with water, that ye may drink, both
ye, and your cattle, and your beasts. And this is
but a light thing in the sight of the LORD: he will
deliver the Moabites also into your hand. And ye
shall smite every fenced city, and every choice
city, and shall fell every good tree, and stop all
wells of water, and mar every good piece of land
with stones. And it came to pass in the morning,
when the meat offering was offered, that, behold,
there came water by the way of Edom, and the
country was filled with water. And when all the
Moabites heard that the kings were come up to
fight against them, they gathered all that were
able to put on armour, and upward, and stood in
the border. And they rose up early in the
morning, and the sun shone upon the water, and

the Moabites saw the water on the other side as red as blood:

And they said, This is blood: the kings are surely slain, and they have smitten one another: now therefore, Moab, to the spoil. And when they came to the camp of Israel, the Israelites rose up and smote the Moabites, so that they fled before them: but they went forward smiting the Moabites, even in their country. And they beat down the cities, and on every good piece of land cast every man his stone, and filled it; and they stopped all the wells of water, and felled all the good trees: only in Kirharaseth left they the stones thereof; howbeit the slingers went about it, and smote it. And when the king of Moab saw that the battle was too sore for him, he took with him seven hundred men that drew swords, to break through even unto the king of Edom: but they could not. Then he took his eldest son that should have reigned in his stead, and offered him for a burnt offering upon the wall. And there was great indignation against Israel: and they departed from him, and returned to their own land.

Call upon the Lord. Be empowered, quit the pity-party, be strong and believe! So shall it be in the name of JESUS, amen!

You Have the Power to: Rebuild Your Life, Relationships & Marriage

ABOUT THE AUTHOR
M. M. Kirschbaum graduated BSN-Cum Laude from NAU-MN. Has a Medical-Surgical Nursing Certification, recertified-CMSRN (Certified Medical-Surgical Registered Nurse) and inducted into the International Association of Nurses.

www.ingramcontent.com/pod-product-compliance
Lightning Source LLC
Chambersburg PA
CBHW060620030426
42337CB00018B/3127